FOR A TENNIS PLAYER
WHO HAS EVERYTHING

A Funny Tennis Book

Team Golfwell and Bruce Miller JD

i

This is the twelfth book in the series, *For People Who Have Everything.*

Cover by Queen Graphics. All images are from Creative Commons or Shutterstock

ISBN 9798355880316 (KDP paperback)

ISBN 9798356061219 (KDP hardback black & white interior)

ISBN 9798356484551 (KDP hardback color interior)

ISBN 978-1-99-104815-8 (Ingram Spark Hardcover)

ISBN 978-1-99-104816-5 (Ingram Spark Paperback)

ISBN 978-1-99-104817-2 (Ingram Spark EPUB)

Watch out for the 17th match! "Nobody beats Vitas Gerulaitis seventeen times in a row."

    -- Vitas Gerulaitis when he finally beat Jimmy Connors after losing sixteen 16 straight matches.

Doesn't matter...really. "It doesn't matter whether you win or lose until you lose."

    -- Charles Schultz

"Play freely". "I told myself to play freely. That means you play the ball. You don't play the opponent. Be free in your head. Be free in your shots. Go for it. The brave will be rewarded here."

    -- Roger Federer

One for the tennis club bar. After several weeks of trying, Joe finally got a beautiful receptionist at his exclusive tennis club to go out on a date with him. Joe spared no expense wanting to impress this beautiful woman and hired a limo, dressed up sharply, and brought her to the most expensive restaurant in town.

However, she was not impressed, and Joe soon realized she was out of his league and the conversation dwindled during an awfully expensive dinner. Joe could tell she knew she was out of his league too. He excused himself and went to the restroom, but on his way there, he saw the beautiful tennis pro, Maria Sharapova dining with a group of friends. This gave Joe an idea.

"Ms. Sharapova, I'm very sorry to interrupt you but I thought you might help me in a matter of the heart?" The waiter came over, but Maria waved him off and said, "For a matter of the heart, I would love to. How can I help you?"

"See that beautiful woman at that table. I've been lovestruck with her ever since I first saw her. But this is our first date, and nothing is going right. Would you kindly stop by our table and pretend to know me and treat me like an old friend? She's a big fan of yours and it would catapult me to the top of her list, for sure!"

Maria laughed and said, "Sure, why not? Go and sit down and I'll catch her eye and notice you and head straight over to you." Joe couldn't thank her enough and made the trip back to his table. As soon as he sat down, he heard Maria shout, "Joe! Is that really you?"

Joe's date looked up and said, "God! Is that Maria Sharapova!"

Joe casually nodded it was.

Maria approached and said, "Joe, why haven't I've seen you around the golf club?! Where on earth have you been love of my life?! I missed you so, so much! How long has it been? Seems like an eternity!"

Joe waved her off and said, "Listen Maria, I told you before – and I don't know how many times – but we're not getting back together! I wish you the best and please, leave me alone. Okay? Thank you."

Rivalry? "What rivalry? I win all the matches."

—Martina Hingis

You know you're too old to play tennis when…

- When you think the age of 60 might be the new 40, but 9:00 pm is the new midnight.

There is another player even louder. Michelle Larcher de Brito yells out on shots at 109 dB! She was formerly ranked as the number one tennis player in Portugal.

Michelle Larcher de Brito

Her coach, Nick Bollettieri, trained her and other players who yell loudly with their shots. Mr. Bollettieri has been criticized for coaching his players to yell out as it seems unfair.

He states, "My staff and I have never taught intentionally yelling as a distraction. It's not something done deliberately to hurt or to get an advantage over their opponents." [1]

Nick pointed out "Players on both the men's and women's tours do grunts when hitting a shot. It's not up to me but up to the rules committee to do something eventually about that."

Michelle Larcher de Brito says she has a right to yell out,

"Nobody can tell me to stop a yell or grunting. Tennis is an individual sport and I'm an individual player. If they must fine me, go ahead. After all I'd rather get fined than lose a match because I had to stop yelling or grunting."

She goes on to say, "If yelling or grunting has inconvenienced the other player, there's nothing I can really do about it, because I don't really want to change anything. I'm here to win. That's simply it. If people don't like my yelling or grunting they can always leave." [2]

The Center for Disease Control (CDC) advises that loud noise levels can be harmful. They explain that a whisper is usually 30 dB, normal talking is about 60 dB, and a normal motorcycle engine is about 95 dB?

The bad part is (and it's good advice as well) that the CDC advises noise above 70 dB over a prolonged period will likely damage hearing and anything above 120 dB can cause immediate harm to your hearing ability. [3] Maria and Michelle are almost getting to that level, and it would be tough to play tennis with earplugs especially when you are listening for the calls from the umpire and line judges.

What do you do? What should you do if you're sitting on a bench ready to play with your partner and waiting for the court to clear, and an unwanted, strange, and odd-looking player sits down next to you?

Silently and slowly put your sunglasses on and stare straight ahead and quietly say, "Did you bring the money?"

The best. "I am the best tennis player who cannot play tennis."

-- Ion Tiriac, former Grand Slam winner and top 10 player on the ATP tour and president of the Romanian Tennis Federation.

Ion Tiriac

Old injury. Three guys were volleying back and forth waiting for Joe who they could see in the distance limping as he walked toward them for their usual doubles match.

"Why are you limping Joe?" Asked one of them as he reached down to pick up a ball on the court.

"It's an old football injury."

"I didn't know you played football, Joe?"

"Oh, I don't. I hurt my foot last year when I lost $1,000 on the Superbowl and put my foot through the TV."

Just one single shot. "I submit that tennis is the most beautiful sport there is and the most demanding. It requires body control, hand-eye coordination, quickness, flat-out speed, endurance, and that weird mix of caution and abandon we call courage. It also requires smarts. Just one single shot in one exchange in one point of a high-level match is a nightmare of mechanical variables."

-- David Foster Wallace, Author

An unusual place to play tennis. Want a unique experience at the most unique tennis club in the big apple? Anyone can play at the New York City Vanderbilt Tennis Club, located inside Grand Central Terminal, on the 4th floor. It's open to the public and you can find it at 15 Vanderbilt Avenue - 4th Floor, NY 10017. [4]

New York City Vanderbilt Tennis Club

World record – Fastest Serve!

The fasted serve recorded in history was served by Australian Sam Groth registered at 163.4 mph (263.4 kph) in Busan, Korea. That took place during the second round of the tournament but unfortunately, Sam lost that match 3-6, 4-6 to Belarussian, Uladzimir Ignatik. [5]

The fastest female service ever recorded was by Germany's Sabine Lisicki who reportedly hit a serve at 210 km/h—the fastest ever recorded in women's tennis. [6]

A very strong and well-coordinated player named, Georgina Garcia Pérez hit a serve that reached 220 km/h (136.7 mph) 2018 Hungarian Ladies Open. [7]

Tennis. "Tennis is the most perfect combination of athleticism, artistry, power, style, and wit. A beautiful game, but one so remorselessly travestied by the passage of time."

— Martin Amis, British novelist

Best hospitality. What sport do restaurant waiters and waitresses play extremely well?

A. Tennis - because they serve so well.

Need other people. "Trying to learn to be a good is like playing tennis against a wall. You can only be a good man, and a competent, capable, interesting and lovable man, when you're doing it for, or with, other people."

-- A. A. Gill, British journalist

Slowest ace ever. Maxime Cressy who has one of the fastest serves on the ATP tour, also hit what many believe is the slowest ace ever.

He produced an unusual slow ace in his first-round match against Christopher Eubanks at the Indian Wells Masters on

Thursday when he produced one of the most unorthodox aces ever seen on a tennis court.

He was up 30-0 in the eighth game of the second set, and Cressy apparently didn't hit the serve as he intended, and the ball looped high off his racket with a sharp hooking curve that just went over the net and bounced sideways.

His opponent tried to return it but was unable to reach it.

You can view a video of that super slow ace here > https://www.youtube.com/watch?v=rCKWA2BLFO4 [8]

Really? "Tennis is certainly a very polite game tennis. The main word seems to be 'Sorry' and in addition to that, players show admiration of each other's play as they face each other across the net and do that frequently as much as the ball crosses the net."

-- James Matthew Barrie, Novelist

How far do you run in a match? During the average match, a player runs up, back, sideways, etc:, for about 3 miles on a regulation-sized court at varying speeds.

Tennis Rule Quiz Question #1

It's a cold day outside, and a player has a runny nose and wipes his nose with the tennis ball. Is that a violation of the rules?

A. Yes, because that is unsanitary.

B. No, people sometimes get runny noses and if it's unintentional then it's okay.

C. Yes since it's changing the texture of the tennis ball like throwing a spitball in baseball.

(The answer is on page 99)

Fuzzy ball. "In tennis the addict moves about a hard rectangle and seeks to ambush a fuzzy ball with a modified snow-shoe."

-- Elliott Chaze, journalist

Life is like a game of tennis. "As in life, you must fight hard to win every point and no matter how hard you try it turns out that sometimes you win and sometimes you lose. And it's the fear of being defeated or not achieving that appears to inspire us to work hard, just like tennis."

-- Anon.

Origins of tennis. It's not exactly certain who invented tennis. There was an order of Monks in the 11th or 12th century who hit a ball back and forth in the courtyard over a string in the center using only their hands.

But the monks found their hands would swell and they came up with the name "jeu de paume" which means "game of the palm."

To ease swelling they began to wear gloves that were webbed and eventually attached a handle to the webbed glove using that to hit the ball over the string in the courtyard.

Gloves with a handle attached were the forerunners of rackets and racquets were used in the late 16th century.

In the late 1800s, Major Walter Clopton Wingfield wrote a book of tennis rules and patented his game in 1874. [9]

In 1875, J. M. Heathcote, a well-known tennis player developed a rubber tennis ball covered with flannel. [10]

Tennis began in the US around the same time in the 1870s. at the Staten Island Cricket and Baseball Club. [11]

The first women's championship began in 1884 at Wimbledon and the women players were in long dresses.

Long dresses were worn at Wimbledon

Foot doctor. I had a one-sided match with my chiropodist and beat him soundly. Despite the bad loss, he was cheerful through the match, and I thought to myself, this man knows how to deal with de feet.

No vax for me. There was a lot of controversy on Novak Djokovic's refusal to take the Coronavirus vaccine. He's developed a nickname, "Novax" Djokovic.

Olympic gold – Williams sisters. Venus and Serena Williams were the first sisters to win Olympic gold medals in doubles tennis. They first won an Olympic gold medal in the Sydney 2000 Olympics and won gold two more times too in Beijing 2008 and London 2012. In effect they showed the world they were not only the best in the world in 2000 but did it repeatedly eight and twelve years later.

Venus won singles gold in 2000 and Serena won single golf in 2012. Amazing!

A mental game. "Tennis is a mental game and besides having to have a great deal of physical skill, you must be a good thinker. If you're not thinking good thoughts and positive thoughts, you win or lose the match before you even go out there."

—Venus Williams

Soars through the air.

The yellow ball soars through the air

From whence it came I do not care

And with a great, tremendous whack

I send it soaring, soaring back.

-- Anon.

Gladiators. "Tennis players we're always playing in center courts that feel like ancient fighting arenas. When we get on the court and the crowd cheers your name to show you great tribute – it's like you're a gladiator in the arena.

Everyone is cheering – and you're fighting, you're screaming, and during your strokes – it feels like you're an animal, fighting for your life."

—Novak Djokovic

The World's Oldest Tennis Court is still being used.

The oldest tennis court in the world is in London called the Hampton Court Palace London royal tennis court. This court was built in the early 1500s.

Henry VIII loved tennis. There is a legend he was given the news of Queen Anne Boleyn's execution while he was playing tennis on Hampton court.

Hampton Court Palace London royal tennis court

That's a lot of balls! Have you ever wondered how many tennis balls are manufactured every year?

A. 325,000,000. [12]

Yellow balls? Have you ever wondered who thought of making tennis balls yellow? In 1986 yellow tennis balls began being used. Yellow balls were first used at Wimbledon since officials believed that a yellow ball would be easier for TV viewers.

Where did the term "love" come from? A. No one really knows. The word "love" is thought to have come from the French word "l'oeuf" meaning "egg," since an egg is shaped like a zero.

Others say the term "love" came from the Dutch saying, "iets voor lof doen," which means "there's no stake in the game."

No hate – be cool. "Keep an even tempo. You don't have to hate your opponents to beat them."

-- Kim Clijsters

The irony of it all. "I hate to lose more than I love to win and to win more, having experience is a great advantage. The irony of it all is that when you get the experience, you're too damned old to do anything about it."

-- Jimmy Connors

How did scoring terms start? Why is the score kept 15-30-40?

The origin of the scoring system of 15, 30, and 40 is unclear but most believe it is based on a clock face where the first quarter hour is 15, the second quarter is 30 and the last quarter is 45. But since 45 was too long to say, it was shortened to 40.

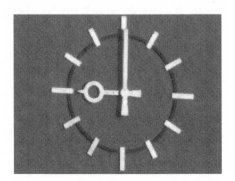

Good old Joe.

A businessman rushed out into the street and just managed to hail a cab going by. *That's lucky* he thought and got in the cab.

"Well, that's timing!" the cabby said. "You're like Joe."

"Who?"

"Joe Blow. Joe's was a guy who did it all right," the driver said. "You know it's just like you hail a cab and there's one that pulls right up to you when you need one. Well, that would have happened just like that to Joe every single time."

"No way!" the man said to the driver. "Everyone has problems. You can't be lucky all the time."

"Not Joe! He was a terrific athlete. He could have been a professional tennis player and gone on the pro tour in tennis."

"Oh, Joe was really something, huh?"

"Yes he sure was," continued the cabby. "He could beat everyone in our tennis club, had a blazing serve. He also had a photographic memory, and he could remember everybody's birthday or anniversary. He was a wine connoisseur and knew all about wines. What a handyman too! He could fix anything. He simply did everything right."

"I can see why you remember him," the man said.

The talkative cabby continued. "Not like me. I try to change a fuse and get a shock and then the whole neighborhood blacks out."

"Did you play tennis against him? the man asked.

"Never did. But some say Joe could hit a forehand so fast it was hard to see the ball! And, I never actually met Joe," said the cabby.

"Well, how the hell do you know so much about him?"

"He slipped on a tennis ball that rolled into the court he was playing on, and he hit his head on the net post, and I married his widow."

Beer. "If I hold the racket this way, I won't have a free hand to hold the beer."

-- Billy Carter (brother of former US President, Jimmy Carter, and creator of "Billy Beer"), while he was being taught how to do a two-handed backhand shot.

When does a new ball lose its bounce? Balls lose their bounce very quickly and start to lose their bounce when you hear the "pssst" opening the can. [13]

Quality regulation tennis balls are kept under a pressure of 2 atmospheres in a sealed can.

Normally the tennis balls that most of us use will last anywhere between 1-4 weeks of light to moderate play.

In competitive tennis, a pressurized set of tennis balls might last only 1-3 hours.

Dad joke. Knock - Knock.

Who's there?

Tennis!

Tennis who?

Tennis four plus six!

How to evaluate a ball's bounce. Balls can be evaluated to determine their bounce by dropping them from a height of 8.333 feet or 254 cm on concrete and they should bounce up between 4.41 to 4.83 feet or 135 and 147 cm. The temperature for the test should be around 68 F degrees or 20 degrees. The test should be done at sea level with 60% humidity. [14]

End of match. When does a tennis match end in the UK?

A. When it's Wimble-DONE

Tennis Rule Quiz Question #2.

You play a drop shot that just gets over the net and your opponent returns it but in doing so, his visor inadvertently touches the net while lunging for the ball. What is the ruling?

A. You win the point because no part of the physical person's body, racket, equipment, or apparel can touch the net.

B. The ball is still in play.

C. No violation since only parts of the bodies can't contact the net and the brim of the visor is not part of the body.

(The answer is on p 99)

Librarians. Why do librarians hate tennis?

A. Too much racket.

What's the score? My wife was upset since I played tennis so much and in addition to that she told me, "I have of 14 other reasons to leave you; besides the fact you play tennis so much!"

I replied, "That's 15 love!"

The best recognition. "You'll hear a lot of applause, cheers, or even loud yells in your life, but none will mean more to you (as it did to me) than a genuine round of applause from your peers.

"I hope each of you get to experience that sometime in your lives."

-- Andre Agassi.

Court adjustment. "I'd just as soon play tennis with the net down."

-- Robert Frost

Getting married. The groom-to-be is next to his bride-to-be at the church altar. The minister greets them and tells them to take a deep breath. As the bride exhales, she notices his tennis racket and bag, two cans of balls, and his tennis clothes draped over the bag off to the side near the door.

"That's your tennis stuff, isn't it?"

"Yes, it is."

"What is that doing here?!" She asks.

 "This isn't going to take all day, is it?"

Going it alone. "It's a lonely game that is one-on-one out there, man. You can't hide and you can't pass the ball."

— Pete Sampras

Ever have 105 points without one unforced error? That many points with no unforced errors? It makes you wonder who did that and who did he play against and where?

Roger Federer did that by having a total of 105 points and in getting those points he had no unforced errors during the 2007

US Open over the last two sets in a three-set match. He won an incredible 105 points without committing a single unforced error.

Was this against a novice? No, his opponent was John Isner - believe it or not!

Ever miss 9000 shots? "I've missed more than 9000 shots in my career. I've lost nearly 300 games. I've been trusted to take the game winning shot and missed the shot 26 times. I've failed many, many times in my life. And that is exactly why I succeed."

That's an amazing positive attitude that can be applied to any sport especially tennis where serves and shots can be missed by slight fractions of an inch.

    -- Michael Jordan

Winning. "A column of ants began to follow me onto the tennis court. Because I would not step on them, I lost the match. But I won with God."

    -- Peter Burwash (1945 - 2022) Canadian tennis player and coach.

Art and an act. It was an art and an act. It was part of my armory. I felt if my opponent didn't know what I was thinking then I was invisible.

-- Bjorn Borg

Longest tennis match ever. The ball may have been bouncing much more than the 20 minutes average when John Isner played Nicolas Mahut in the longest tennis match in history when they played 5 sets over three days that included a 138-point tiebreaker.

It took 11 hours and five minutes, and this match went on record as the longest tennis match ever. It was a match played in the first round at Wimbledon in 2010.

They were even in sets after four sets and the match was stopped because of darkness. They resumed the next day, and they were still tied 47 – 47 in games in the fifth set when the scoreboard stopped working.

On the third day, Isner finally won after breaking serve and holding his own serve with a final winning score of 6-4, 3-6, 6-7, 7-6, 70-68.

Mermaids. Why don't mermaids play tennis?

A. They are afraid of being caught in the net.

Looking for a highly romantic place to play?

No place like Paris, the City of Love. This court has an amazing view of the Eiffel Tower. [15]   Entirely renovated in 2000 and built in 1924, the building is listed as a historic monument of the city of Paris, and it has kept its former glory.

It's located above the classy Aston Martin garage on the border of the 7th and 15th arrondissements. The club features a new greenset court covered by a wooden honeycomb structure, and from the court you can walk into open terraces offering a highly romantic panorama of the Eiffel Tower, the Invalides and the rooftops of Paris.

The Eiffel Tower is ranked as the 7th most visited monument in the world with seven million visitors per year. [16] (The forbidden city in China is #1 with 17,000,000 visits per year. But you can't play tennis in the Forbidden City as far as we know).

If you have ever dreamed of playing tennis in a unique and atypical place, try the TENNIS DE LA CAVALERIE Club which will delight you with its architecture, its simplicity and the charm of yesteryear in the city of love.

Only a very short walk to the Eiffel Tower, the original building was designed by famous French architect named R. Farradèche and received national monument status in 1986.

Wear sunglasses when you pass through the gorgeous James Bondish Aston Martin dealership on the first floor. Take the ancient elevator to the 7th floor where the club is located.

The locker rooms are very fashionable like the best tennis clubs in France.

There is a balcony next to the locker rooms on the 7th floor where you can take in the view of the Eiffel Tower across the magnificent park Champ de Mars. On the right day, it most likely will take your breath away. [17]

Tennis de la Cavalerie Club

Still playing. Joe was 75 years old and extremely wealthy. His wife had died years ago, and he belonged to an expensive and very exclusive tennis club. He played well. His knees and hips were fine, and he was lean and mean on the court.

One day, he walked into the tennis clubhouse bar with a gorgeous and extremely sexy 22-year-old blonde. They turned everyone's heads as they strolled into the bar. She was draping herself all over Joe giving him her complete and undivided attention.

His friends at the club were astonished. They couldn't believe their eyes! When the blonde got up to visit the ladies' room, they asked Joe, "How the hell did you manage to get her as your girlfriend?"

"Oh, she's not my girlfriend, Joe replied, "She's my wife!"

They couldn't believe it and one asked, "Married? Wow! How did you do that?"

"Well, truth be told, I lied a bit about my age."

"What? Oooh, I see, you're trying to tell us you told her you were only 50 and that beautiful creature believed you?"

Joe smiled and said, "Not at all! I told her I was 95!"

Amazing Steffi Graff. She is the only player, male or female, to have won each major tournament at least four times.

She was also ranked as the number one female tennis player for 377 weeks.

Steffi lives in Las Vegas with her husband Andre Agassi. Andre founded the Andre Agassi Charitable Foundation raising millions of dollars for disadvantaged, abused, or disabled children in Nevada.

They have a son, Jaden Agassi, 6' 3" and 195 lbs. who has turned out to be a powerful baseball pitcher for the University of Southern California baseball time. He recently entered the NCAA transfer portal.

Steffi Graf

The court is my home.

When I play tennis,

no matter what,

it brings out my deepest passion, fire, drive, and desire.

after I step foot on that magical court.

It is now my home,

I do not want to leave.

I spend every spare second of my time on that court with a racket in hand,

and a bucket of balls making irreplaceable memories.

The court is my home.

That feeling is what passion is.

So, play with love, passion, and fire and know you are making the best memories of your life.

No matter the outcome of your match, or how bad you played,

This is tennis.

A tradition that forms memories.

      -- Anon.

We're from the ghetto. "Venus is a ghetto Cinderella. People from the ghetto don't get nervous."

"There's no place rougher in the world. The ghetto will make you rough, it'll make you tough, it'll make you strong.

-- Richard Williams, "King Richard". Coach and father of Venus and Serena.

No barriers "The tennis ball doesn't know how old I am. The ball doesn't know if I'm a man or a woman or if I come from a communist country or not. Sport has always broken down these barriers."

-- Martina Navratilova

Martina Navratilova

When did tennis balls start being packaged in a can?

As the tennis ball evolved over the years, they were packaged in wrapped paper and paperboard boxes. [18]

In 1925, Wilson-Western Sporting Goods Company began to pack them and sell them in cardboard tubes.

The first canned tennis balls happened in 1926 when the Pennsylvania Rubber Company sold them in a sealed pressurized metal tube that held three balls. There was no pull tab and a can opener or church key had to be used to open them.

In the 1980s, tennis balls were put into plastic cans with a full-top pull-tab seal and plastic lid that would fit three or four balls per can. [19]

Tennis Quiz Question #3.

It's a close match. After you smash a forehand you shout out a little banter, "You're not returning this one!"

You're just letting off a little steam and you want to let him know he's not going to beat you. And you're just releasing stress trying to keep yourself relaxed, so no violation, correct?

A. Banter is allowed.

B. It's bad etiquette but no rule violation.

C. If it's deliberate the opponent wins the point.

(*The answer is on p. 99*)

Fail better. "As a tennis player, you must get used to losing every week. Unless you win the tournament, you always go home as a loser.

"But you must take the positive out of a defeat and go back to work. You have to improve to fail better."

-- Stan Wawrinka

Stan's positive philosophy is a great example. That philosophy has certainly served him very well in his career having won over 35 million dollars in prize money alone. [20]

Tenez and Novak the polyglot. The English word, "Tennis" comes from the Anglo-Norman term "Tenez."

It's called "tenis" in Spanish, "tenisas" in Lithuanian, "ithenisi" in Zulu, "wangqui" in Chinese, "tenisi" in Samoan, "tenisu" in Japanese, but for the most part, it sounds like the word tennis in most every language.

Novak Djokovic, besides being one of the greatest to play in the game, is peculiarly multi-lingual. Novak is fluent in 11 different languages. Those are his native Serbian, English, French, Chinese, German, Italian, Spanish, Arabic, Russian, Portuguese, and Japanese. That's amazing!

80% of all the people in the world speak those languages so he can speak almost all the languages in the countries he plays tennis in around the world. Check Novak out on YouTube [21] (https://www.youtube.com/watch?v=sUtQadqgxZo).

Sportsmanship. Most people go along with the often-said adage, "When you lose, say little. When you win, say less."

Jim Courier, former World No. 1, has his own definition of sportsmanship. Jim said it's when a player walks off the court and you can't tell whether he won or lost, and in either event, he carries himself with pride."

Whiff. If a baseball player whiffs, it's a strike.

If a golfer completely misses the ball, it counts as a stroke.

In hockey, a whiff is called fanning on the puck.

In tennis missing the ball completely when you attempt a service, is a fault.

What about missing an overhead? Most of us know that it can be embarrassing and funny too especially if you miss it and the ball lands on your head!

Most misses are caused by trying to hit down on the ball when you must hit an overhead. One way to practice an effective way of hitting overheads is to first get in the right position and be ready. Try turning your body sideways while bringing your racket behind your back using a hammer grip.

Then point your other hand up toward the sky. When you do this you will be keeping your body open and, at the same time, your racket shoulder lowered.

Then swing your racket straight up toward the sky with your arm fully extended and contact the ball at a 60-degree angle.

Where did the tiebreaker idea come from? The tiebreaker was created by a man named James "Jimmy" Van Alen in 1965. Mr. Van Alen was an American tennis official and a poet, musician, publisher, civic leader, and raconteur. [22]

He was best known for establishing the International Tennis Hall of Fame. Jimmy lived to be 88 years old and died in 1991.

Just two days after his death, Stefan Edberg was playing in a Wimbledon semifinal and lost to Michael Stich in an exceptionally long match that went 6–4, 6–7 (5), 6–7 (5), 6–7 (2). When Stefan heard of Jimmy's passing, he said, "If he hadn't lived, Michael and I might still be out there playing."

"You cannot be serious" paid off years later. John McEnroe said those words on June 22, 1981, to the chair umpire at Wimbledon when playing Tom Gullikson and was fined 750 pounds and almost thrown out of the tournament

(which he ultimately won in a rematch final over Bjorn Borg who won the year before).

After telling the referee those words, John continued his questioning, "You can't be serious, man, you cannot be serious! That ball was on the line, the chalk flew up! It was clearly in. How can you possibly call that out?"

When asked about it today, John mentions he was paid bonuses every time he was asked to repeat those infamous words that questioned authority.

"I'd call it a mixed blessing but more positive than negative, ironically. It was the only time I said it in my 15-year career and then suddenly when I played on the Seniors' Tour, I got paid a bonus if I said it."

John is amazed that the simple remark he said to the umpire in 1981 followed him throughout his career. [23]

They had a well-known rivalry that some referred to as "Fire and Ice" because of their playing styles. They played against each other 14 times on the regular tennis tour with each of them winning 7 times.

They were called "Fire and Ice" because of their manner on the court with McEnroe being loud and overtly assertive while Borg was generally very cool and almost emotionless. for his court-side tantrums.

By the way, rivals John and Bjorn later became friends off the court. Bjorn said, "We talk and see one another from time to time and that's something you don't find very often in competitive sports. It's because we understand the nature of each other."

John McEnroe and Bjorn Borg

An observation from Rod. "The nature of tennis is like a happily married couple playing a mixed doubles game that turns into a shouting session or scene from the Broadway play, "Who's Afraid of Virginia Woolf."

-- Rod Laver

Why the pineapple? A pineapple was put at the top of the Wimbledon men's singles trophy, but why is unclear.

Some say, after Christopher Columbus found Plymouth Rock, he brought a pineapple back, but the pineapple couldn't be grown in Europe. It was very special if you happened to have one and only the very wealthy had pineapple.

Also, English sailors would place a pineapple outside their door after returning home from a long voyage. All in all, pineapples were very special and made excellent prizes in the early days of Wimbledon in the late 19th century.

Novak Djokovic holding Wimbledon Trophy with pineapple on top

Don't try too hard. "The player of the inner game comes to value the art of relaxed concentration above all other skills. Discovering self-confidence, he learns that the secret to winning any game lies in not trying too hard."

— W. Timothy Gallwey, The Inner Game of Tennis: The Classic Guide to the Mental Side of Peak Performance

What was the shortest 5-set men's match? Bill
Tilden was the most prominent player in the 1920s. In 1927 the US formed a team to play a Great Britain team before the Wimbledon Tournament was to take place.

Bill played UK's D M Greig, in the opening match. Greig was a last-minute replacement.

Most say, Mr. Greig tried his hardest and if you've ever felt you're playing someone way above your league, he certainly did.

Bill won the first and second sets 6-0, 6-0, and it was 4-0 in the third set before Bill lost two games in the set before winning the third set 6-2.

The match lasted an amazing 22 minutes and that record remains today as the fastest best of five-set match ever.

Bill Tilden

Lessons we learn about life from tennis.

Keep your eye on the ball.

Commit to following through.

Every game begins with love.

Learn from losses.

Each point is a new opportunity.

Believe in yourself.

Depressed players. There is an online website dedicated only to depressed tennis players…but the servers are currently down…

A father's advice. A Father pulled his son aside, "We need to have a talk son. In the years to come, you will have strong desires you haven't ever had before. Your heart will be pounding, your hands sweaty and you'll be totally consumed with passion."

"What are you saying, Dad? I think I know all that stuff."

"Please understand these feelings are perfectly normal. It's called tennis."

A King tragically blocked by...tennis balls.

Scotland's King James I enjoyed tennis but kept losing tennis balls that rolled in the sewage drain at the court at Blackfriars Monastery. So, he ordered that the drains be blocked.

Recently thereafter, on an evening in February 1437, James and the Queen were in their rooms and separated from most of their servants when a group of assassins (thought to be about 30) entered led by Robert Graham.

King James was awoken and had time to hide in a sewer tunnel that had an exit that would enable him to escape, but that sewer tunnel was the same tunnel he had ordered to be blocked off because he kept losing tennis balls down them and he was unfortunately trapped and murdered. [24]

Dating Tennis players. Ever Date a Tennis Player?

Be wary. Love means nothing to them.

Tennis Quiz Question #4.

Your opponent clearly overhits the ball and it's bee-lining off the court and impossible to land inbounds. So, you catch it before it lands.

You explain you don't want to go chasing another wild shot. Violation?

A. No violation.

B. The ball must bounce first.

C. You win the point since it was obviously going out.

(The answer is on p. 99)

Quote about the real nature of tennis. "Why has bashing and slamming a tennis ball with a racquet become such an enjoyable sport giving pleasure for so many of us?"

"It seems clear to me that a primary attraction of the sport is the opportunity it gives to release a great deal of aggression physically without being arrested for felonious assault."

-- Nat Hentoff, Syndicated columnist

Reality strikes. Middle-aged Joe was told by his doctor to start playing a sport, so he decided to take up tennis.

After buying a racket, shoes, balls, and tennis attire, and joining a club, Joe's wife asked him how he was coming along.

"Well, it is interesting and going okay for now. I love to get on the court and watch my opponent send the ball back to me super-fast! I think 'Sprint! Dash! To the corner! Back hand! Smash! Overhead!'"

"Really? What happens then?" his wife asks.

"Then my body says, 'What the hell? Me? You gotta be kidding!'"

Fast service at a dinner party. I went to a fancy dinner party dressed as a tennis ball.

I got served straight away.

Peace Prize. "I was walking through the park on my way to the court and saw 2 dogs fighting. So, I took out a tennis ball and shouted 'Fetch!' and threw a tennis ball into a large bush. Both immediately stopped fighting and ran for the ball.

"Moments later they returned but didn't have my ball. And they left after a while not fighting anymore.

"So, I deserve a "No ball peace prize."

Tennis or basketball? After I played tennis for a while I got totally frustrated and decided to play basketball. I should have known I'd be better at basketball since I get nothing but net at both!

Naked tennis. Why did the blonde enter the tennis courts naked?

Because the sign said, "Tennis shoes only."

Tennis scorekeepers. Q. What's the difference between a waiter and a scorekeeper at a tennis match?

A. One sets tables, and the other tables sets.

Walking the dog. Joe told me when he was walking his dog today that his dog was able to retrieve a tennis ball the dog heard bounce 2 miles away. But that sounds far-fetched!

Dating a tennis player. Where did the tennis couple go on their date?

A. The Tennis Ball.

Youngest player to win the US Open. Carlos Alcaraz won the 2022 US Open and because of that and his other wins, he became the youngest man ever to be ranked world No. 1 by the ATP, at 19 years and a little over 4 months old.

Carlos Alcaraz Garfia is 6'1" tall and weighs 160 lbs. He began playing tennis at the age of 4 and his father was a Spanish tennis academy director.

His agent, Albert Molina (who also represented David Ferrer) said, "I was following him a lot in the early years. He was just a skinny kid"

His parents allowed Molina to coach him despite thinking he was still too young when Carlos was about 12 years old. [25]

He was only 19 when he defeated his lifelong idol, Rafael Nadal in the quarterfinals to become the first teenager ever to beat Rafael on clay. [26]

Then he beat top-seeded Djokovic in the semifinals and was the youngest player to win a match against Novak.

In the final, Carlos beat second seeded and defending champion Alexander Zverev. Very remarkable indeed and hopefully a sign of a new rising star!

Carlos has said he believes his playing style is like the great Roger Federer who frequently comes to the net and uses drop shots. He is very strong from the baseline and has a blistering forehand and has hit frequent winners from the baseline. And he can hit an excellent drop shot.

Carlos has the same hobby as Rafa and that's golf.

This young man is bound to break more records and has a bright future.

It seems it's coming around for Carlos just as Roger Federer said years ago about his own career, "Success is a great thing because it means you've taken a step forward and gives you a sense of pride. That gives you confidence and experience and that is a positive circle."

Carlos Alcaraz Garfia

Tennis excuses.

- My back hurts from carrying my partner.

- I play better with a drink in me.

- They must have played in college.

- Are you sure it was out?

- Didn't it double bounce?

- I forgot my sunglasses.

- All they did was lob!

- I lost the ball in the sun.

- The ball took a strange bounce.

- They were backboards!

- Damn shoulder.

- Damn knee.

- Damn tennis elbow!

- My strings are too loose.

- My strings are too tight.

- I need new strings!

"Mon Dieu! How much did we pay for these tickets!?

Shortest Grand Slam final ever. In 1988, Steffi Graf defeated Natasha Zvereva in the French Open final and blanked her 6–0, 6–0.

The official time of the match was 34 minutes, but the actual playing time of the match was 32 minutes. Nine minutes after the match started, it started to rain and there was a rain break for a bit, then the match was concluded 23 minutes later totaling 32 minutes playing time.

It is also the only "double bagel" and completely one-sided Grand Slam singles final of the Open Era, and only the second double bagel in the history of tennis (the other being in 1911 at Wimbledon). [27]

Being a winner. "Some people say I have attitude — maybe I do — but I think you must have attitude. You must have an attitude and the confidence to believe in yourself when no one else does. If you can do that you are a winner already."

-- Venus Williams

Find another partner. Joe came home early from tennis. His wife is surprised. "Why are you home? What happened?"

Pete and I aren't playing tennis with each other anymore."

"But you've played together for years?"

"I know, I know, Joe said.

"Why?"

"Well, would you play with someone who cheats, has a foul mouth, smashes his racket, call balls out when they're clearly in, and doesn't pay the wager when he loses?"

"No way! That's terrible!"

"Well, neither will Pete!"

Groaners. Tennis shoes? I was taking my kids out to play a bit of tennis and they were talking up a storm when my wife asked, "Do you have tennis shoes?"

I just told her, "No, I only have 9 issues."

Too old? Me too old? I couldn't believe my wife said she's had enough and is leaving me because I'm totally obsessed with tennis – and I'm too old.

I replied, "I'm only 40 love."

How true! "There's an old saying that goes something like, it's not whether you win or lose that matters. That, I guess, is sportsmanship. But I think whoever said that was a player who probably lost."

-- Martina Navratilova

First serve. My wife told me to get the car out of the garage and that we must leave right now and get to the tennis courts before they open.

I asked, "Why so early?"

She said, "It's first come first serve!

The all-white rule? My underwear too? A few female Wimbledon stars were forced to go braless during the tournament due to the all-white rule when colored undergarments disrupted the all-white color.

Wimbledon has a strict all-white dress code and players now understand that applies to underwear as well. Colored underwear is outlawed if it can be seen during play (including being seen because of sweating).

The rules do allow a single trim of color not wider than 1 cm.

That is a very thin line so to be proper Venus Williams changed her bra mid-match after several complaints were made by the Wimbledon hierarchy.

Nick Kyrgios, an overly entertaining player, who makes it known no one tells him what to do wore red trainers on Wimbledon's Centre Court.

There have been times the women players had to remove their bras. The officials could see that they had a slight color, and they couldn't wear them. That, of course, made the men pay much more attention than normal watching play when the bras were removed.

A former Wimbledon Champion, Pat Cash told the media, that in his opinion it got almost ridiculous when the girls had to remove undergarments that only had very slight colors. And the girls who didn't have time to find an all-white sports bra had to go without them.

There is a tradition and Venus Williams being a good sport commented that the all-white rule does give the tournament a certain uniqueness and a shiny bright look.

It's not simple. "It's hard for most people to imagine tennis is a creative process. On the surface, it seems to the spectator that it's just an athletic matter of hitting the ball consistently well within the boundaries of the court. But that superficial analysis is just as specious as thinking that the difficulty in portraying King Lear on stage is learning all the lines."

-- Virginia Wade

Everyone is fit. "Tennis is truly a mental game since when you play professionally, it's the mental game that really matters as most every player is able to hit great forehands and backhands."

-- Novak Djokovic

From the Highest Court. "When I was 40, my doctor told me that a man in his 40s shouldn't play tennis. So, I heeded his advice carefully and could hardly wait until I reached 50 to start again."

-- Hugo L. Black, (1876 – 1971) Former US Supreme Court Justice.

New Tennis Tour. With due respect to Native Americans, it's been reported that American Indians are considering establishing their own professional tennis tournaments.

They will provide accommodations at no cost to players from other tribes. They plan to call it, "A Free Tee Pee Tour."

Talk about a high lob? The organizers for the Dubai Duty-Free Men's Tennis Open in 2005 invited Roger Federer and Andre Agassi to play a promotional match on the Burj Al Arab helipad that they converted temporarily into a tennis court.

The helipad is at an altitude of 656 feet high and the views are truly amazing.

Burj Al Arab Helipad (Dubai)

Two rackets started dating. Q. Why did two tennis rackets stop dating?

A. One of them found out the other one was just stringing her along without any real plans to tie the knot.

Largest Tennis Stadiums. The Arthur Ashe Stadium in New York City is the world's largest tennis stadium. [28]

Arthur Ashe Stadium, NYC

The top 5 largest venues where tennis is played are:

1. The largest is the Arthur Ashe Stadium, New York City, with a capacity of 23,771.

2. Sydney Super Dome, Sydney, has a capacity of 18,200.

3. O2 Arena London has a capacity of 17,500.

4. The Indian Wells Tennis Garden (Stadium 1) in Indian Wells, CA has a capacity of 16,102.

5. Rotterdam Ahoy, Rotterdam, Netherlands, has a capacity of 15,818.

(Wimbledon Centre Court has a capacity of 12,345.)

Tennis Quiz Question #5.

You hit a shot and send your opponent wide, and he hits the ball around the net post instead of over the net to your side of the court. What should you do?

A. Compliment him on his imagination? No way, it's your point.

B. That ball is still in play so hit it back!

C. The ball is only still in play if it was hit around the net on the deuce side of the court.

(The answer is on p. 99)

Hard to retire. "It is very difficult to retire when you do something best. You really don't want to give that up - and for me that's tennis."

> -- Roger Federer

What kind of racket string is recommended?

Talk to your tennis pro about what to use for stringing your racket and knows what your ability is. That's the best way to get the right advice.

If you can't talk to your pro, then generally,

- Beginners usually play with nylon strings (or natural gut if you can afford it).

- Intermediate players usually start to blend with hybrids.

- Professional tennis players usually use 100% polyester although many like the feel of natural gut which is very hard to duplicate.

Regular Sunday doubles. Two couples were playing their regular Sunday mixed-doubles match. However, this Sunday, one of the women had a bad case of excessive flatulence.

Whenever she tried to hit it as hard as the men did, she swung wildly, and half of the time whiffed it, and the other times spun it off the racket frame and trumpeted loud farts swinging with way too much force.

Her husband tried to calm her and being calmer, she tried again. This time she took her eye off the ball and topped the ball off the bottom of her racket only to have it dribble a few feet in front of her. When she did this, she let out another fart only a lot quieter this time.

Exasperated, she said, "I wonder why the ball didn't go very far"

The other gentleman said, "I believe you needed more gas to give it a lot more gas!"

Gender match set number difference.

Q. Why do men play best out of five for matches and women only play best out of three?

A. Women are more efficient.

What tension should rackets be strung to?

Talking to your tennis pro who knows your ability is usually best.

Nylon or natural gut around 50-60lbs is a good base recommended tension.

Polyester usually should be strung lower to avoid arm injuries.

If you can't talk to your pro, then generally (give or take a few pounds),

- Nylon/Gut: 50-62 lbs. (22.5-28kg)
- Hybrid: 46-56 lbs. (21-25.5kg)
- Polyester: 44-54 lbs. (20-24.5kg)

Family. "Family's first. That's what matters most. We realize that our love for our family goes deeper than the tennis game."

-- Serena Williams

LA Tennis. "I was an excellent tennis player when I grew up in Canada, and I was nationally ranked junior player when I was, like, 13. Then I moved to Los Angeles when I was 15, and everyone in L.A. just killed me. I was great in Canada. Not so much in Los Angeles."

-- Matthew Perry

Enlightened. A zookeeper who plays tennis is having problems deciding on a racket. While he's pondering, the director of the zoo approaches him and says, "We need you to move the animals to different cages and be careful transporting them and use the mover's dolly as it's safer to move to wheel them on the dolly, to their new cage."

The Zookeeper says, "No problem."

He goes to the lion cage leads the lion onto the dolly while thinking, "What frame should I use?" and then puts the lion in his new cage.

Then he goes to the tiger cage, gets the tiger and wheels the tiger to another cage while he's muttering to himself, "Tweener or players frame?" and puts the tiger in his new cage.

He then goes to the Llama cage and as he's wheeling the Llama, he's still muttering, "Thick beam or thin beam?"

Suddenly the Llama speaks up and says, "Just use the Prince Original Graphite Oversize, it's the best damn frame ever made."

The zookeeper is shocked that the Llama can talk, but he orders that exact racket, and he plays excellently with it.

Moral: If you seek enlightenment, ask the dollied Llama.

No matter how good you get. "Tennis can get you down since the most depressing thing about it is that no matter how good you think you get, you'll never be as good as a wall."

    -- Mitch Hedberg, Comedian

Brave on the court. "When I am home alone at night that believe it or not, makes me nervous. I will sleep on the sofa since I can't face going to bed. I leave the TV on and turn on all the lights. I'm not very brave about anything in life. But in tennis, yes! In everything else, not very."

--Rafael Nadal

Joy. "Every time I went out on the court, it just gave me such joy to play."

--Evonne Goolagong Cawley, former Aussie No. 1.

Do you remember the battle of the sexes? Bobby Riggs was a former Wimbledon champion but now was 55 years old. He was known to be a true chauvinist and challenged 30-year-old Margaret Court to a singles match and beat her 6-2, 6-1 easily.

Billie Jean King didn't like that. She had been challenged by Bobby, but she declined. Now she wanted the match and changed her mind and Bobby took her on.

The match was played at the Houston Astrodome in 1973 attended by over 30,000 fans and almost 50 million TV viewers.

Bobby made his entrance being wheeled in on a rickshaw pulled by gorgeous women and dressed up as Henry VIII while chewing on a huge bone.

Billie Jean presented Bobby with a piglet for his chauvinism then she let her racket do the talking and beat Bobby 6-4, 6-3, 6-3. Billy Jean won $100,000 for that.

At the interview after the match, Bobby had met his match and then some and was worn out. He kept saying, "I didn't think she was that quick!"

Billie Jean King and Bobby Riggs

No accident. "It's no accident, in my view, that tennis has the language of life with words like advantage, service, fault, break, and love. Those are basic words of everyday existence, and every match seems it is a life in miniature.

"It's the structure of tennis and the way the pieces fit inside one another like Russian dolls, which mimics the structure of our days. Points become games, and games become sets, and sets become tournaments. It's all so tightly connected, and any point can become a turning point.

"All in all, it reminds me of the way seconds become minutes and minutes become hours, and any hour can be our finest. Or darkest. It's our choice."

— Andre Agassi

Bounce the ball. "Though your game might not be the best, you can get on your opponent's nerves by methodically slowly bouncing the ball at least ten times before your serves.

-- Arnold J. Zarett

When you're in the fifth set, this is what it's about. "If you are playing in the fifth set of a match, it's not about tennis anymore. It's about nerves."

-- Boris Becker

Tennis Quiz Question #6.

You serve underhand and your opponent tells you that "you serve like a whimp" and says serving that way is illegal. Is he correct?

A. No. Serving underhand is allowed.

B. You must serve overhand.

C. Serving underhand is legal but not legal in mixed doubles.

(*The answer is on p. 99*)

How you handle it. "If you can reach a point where you can react the same way to the times when you win and the times when you lose, that's a big accomplishment!

"That's because that quality stays with you the rest of your life, and you need that since there's going to be a life after tennis that's a lot longer and perhaps way tougher than your tennis life."

-- Chris Evert

A strange combination. "Tennis is oddly a combination of fast and violent action taking place in an atmosphere of total tranquility."

-- Billie Jean King

What is a hero? "True heroism is remarkably quiet, sober, and very undramatic. It's not the urge or desire to win against all the others no matter what the cost. It's actually the ongoing urge to serve others at whatever cost."

-- Arthur Ashe

Ever done something dumb? Everyone has, of course. In the 2000 Samsung Open in Brighton UK, Goran Ivanisevic, a Croatian player entered the 2000 Samsung Open in Brighton. He was confident going into the tournament being a former runner-up at Wimbledon in 1992, 1994 and 1998. [29]

In a 2nd-round match against South Korea's Hyung-Taik Lee, Goran later said he did not think it would be a difficult match. Then he lost the first set in a close set and smashed his racket in frustration.

He went on to take the second set 7-6 winning the tiebreaker.

Then in the third set, he cracked his racket but continued to play with a cracked racket but threw it away when changing sides.

Then Goran double-faulted giving Lee two break points. Again, Goran smashed his third racket banging on the court.

After he got done smashing his racket, he told the referee he didn't have any more rackets.

The rules provided if you run out of rackets you're done and must retire. Goran became the first player to ever lose a match by not having another racket.

Goran told Associated Press, "At least when I've finished playing tennis, they'll remember me for something...They'll say, 'There's that guy who never won Wimbledon, but he smashed all his rackets and lost a match since he didn't have any more rackets!" [30]

The brighter side of the story is that a year later Goran (with plenty of rackets) won the Wimbledon singles title as a wildcard (and he is the only player to have ever won Wimbledon as a wildcard). At that time, he held a world ranking of 125. [31]

Goran was reported as saying, "As soon as I step on the court I just try to play tennis and don't find excuses. You know, if I lose, I tell myself I just lost because I lost, not because my arm was sore, or any other excuse."

Goran Ivanisevic

You can't touch this! Mark "Flipper" Philippoussis's serve has recorded a personal best 229.0 km/h (142.3 mph) serve. At that time Mark had the biggest serve in the game.

A newspaper tennis columnist challenged Mark to serve to him to see if he could return it as he was doing a feature story on Mark.

To no one's surprise, the reporter couldn't even get his racket on a serve.

After 24 serves, Mark called out, "Last one" and hit a serve making the reporter jump out of the way of the ball coming right at him.

When Mark was interviewed later about how it all went, he said, "I missed him."

Keeping a poker face. "I discovered that the best way to play is without any emotion - well, without any emotion others could see. "Card players do well from having a poker face so opposing players don't know how good or bad their hand was. I believe a deadpan expression works in tennis as well."

      -- Rod Laver

Watch your tongue! Andre Agassi had trouble trying to beat Boris Becker when he first played against him. They developed a rivalry and Boris beat Agassi three times in a row in the first three matches they played against each other.

Agassi was determined to beat him, and he watched the videos of their matches repeatedly. He finally discerned a strange habit of Becker before he served.

It was a subconscious habit of Becker in that every time Becker got ready to serve, he would stick his tongue out. If his tongue came out to the left of his mouth and hung out to the left, his serve would go wide. And if his tongue came out and hung out in the middle of his mouth the ball would stay in the center.

It was that simple. After that in the eleven matches they played Becker won only one match and when Becker retired he had a losing record of 4-10 against Agassi.

In an interview Andre said, "The most awkward thing was not letting Boris know I knew this. I didn't read his serve every time but only chose times when I needed the point. And when I did I didn't have a problem breaking his serve. The hardest thing was hiding the fact I could break it at will. If I let on, he'd just keep his tongue in his mouth."

Andre said he finally did let Boris know. "I told Boris after he retired when I was with him at Oktoberfest, and we had a pint together. When I told him he fell off the chair!

Then he said, 'I used to go home and tell my wife — it's like Andre reads my mind. Little did I know you were just reading my tongue.'" [32]

Alone. "When you play tennis, you're alone. That teaches you about life. You bring your best and make those around you better, too -- helping others in difficult moments."

-- Jurgen Klopp, well-known football manager.

Your real enemy. "Losing is not my enemy, fear of losing is my enemy."

-- Rafael Nadal

Their rackets didn't do the talking this time.

During the Australian Open in 1998, sisters Serena and Venus Williams declared that they could win a match against any man, who is over 200th place in the ATP rating.

That was a bold statement. So, Karsten Braasch, who was ranked 203rd at that time, accepted the challenge.

He won the first set against Venus with a score of 6-2 and the second one against Serena with a score of 6-1.

After the match, Karsten said he didn't really do his best and that he played as a 600th-place player in the ATP rating.

Roger's secret wish. "I would so like to be Lenny Kravitz."

-- Roger Federer

Ghost in a tennis outfit? Really? Casey Batchelor is a successful English model and a TV celebrity. She started with an average background like most of us except her mother Kim is the godmother of Victoria Beckham.

Casey was on the TV show Celebrity Big Brother house.

Casey Batchelor

Casey has made it known she's just a normal person like anyone else. So that seems to make her story even more credible.

Casey was interviewed by a reporter from the Daily Star who reported that in 2014, Casey said she was slapped by a ghost who was angry that she was in his bed. [33]

Casey went to a manor house to celebrate Valentine's day with her partner when she suddenly felt like she was touched by a man while she was asleep.

She woke up and saw a figure of a man wearing an old-fashioned white tennis outfit walking away from her. Casey figured she must be dreaming and went back to sleep.

But then woke up again and saw the man standing next to her bed in the same outfit. Then the ghost said to her, "Move over" and slapped her face. She said the force of the slap moved her face to the side. Groggy, she said she just closed her eyes and fell back to sleep.

When she woke in the morning, there was no ghost. Later the host of the manor told her there have been several ghost sightings over the years of people who used to live there wearing tennis outfits. [34]

Short memory. "Every good tennis player must have a short memory on shots whether they were good or bad."

-- Alexander Zverev

His racket speaks. "I let my racket do the talking. That's just the way I am and how I act all the time. I just go out and try to win tennis matches."

-- Pete Sampras, former No. 1, and 14 major titles (7 Wimbledon titles, 2 Australian Opens and 5 US Open titles).

Pete Sampras

Tennis Quiz Question #7.

You're up at the net and your opponent hits a powerful passing shot you can't reach. Your reflexes cause you to instantly toss your racket at the ball. The ball hits it and miraculously returns the ball back over the net. Your opponent claims the point. Is he correct?

A. No. That is so extraordinary and rare you are entitled to the point.

B. No. The ball hit the racket so that's okay!

C. Sorry, he's right - you can't throw a racket.

(*The answer is on p. 99*)

PS on Question #7. It can be a close call on throwing a racket ask in Question # 7 and you might want to view this interesting video on YouTube here > https://www.youtube.com/watch?v=4P7SO7Oe1Eg

Andy Murray can't control his balls!

There is a rule in tennis that most know that if balls keep falling out of your pocket deliberately, your opponent has the option to claim "hindrance" and that would entitle the opponent to the point.

At Wimbledon in 2012, a ball happened to fall out of Andy's pocket. Andy claimed it wasn't his fault and "was totally beyond his control."

Then during the match, it happened again! Next, (you guessed right) it happened a third time!

The umpire had no other choice due to the number of times the balls fell out that it really wasn't a fluke and really wasn't outside of Andy's control and awarded Andy's opponent two points.

In his next match, he wasn't wearing those shorts and had shorts with much deeper pockets.

Tennis slogans you might not have heard.

- "Here ye, Here ye, order on the Court."

- "Serve, Smash, Win, and love it all."

- Be respectful. "Respect All, Fear None."

- "If it's gonna be, it starts with me."

- "Champions train. Losers complain."

- "Refuse to Lose!"

- "We're not waiters (or waitresses), but boy can we serve!"

- "All it takes is all you've got!"

- "There's no traffic on the extra mile."

- "Our blood, our sweat, your tears."

- "All Out, All Game, All Season."

- "A team above all. Above all, a team."

Very few know this. "Now that I've won a Grand Slam, I know something few people know. That is that a win doesn't feel as good as much as a loss feels bad. And the good feeling doesn't last long as the bad feeling of losing. Not even close."

— Andre Agassi, Open

Hey! I'm trying to play tennis here! Ilie Nastase played a match in the US Open on the old Grandstand court.

During the match, overhead low-flying commercial airliners annoyed him as they were departing LaGuardia and JFK airports.

When you're trying to earn a living you try everything to do that so he requested the chair umpire of his match to call the air traffic controller tower of the airports to reroute the planes so they wouldn't bother those playing important matches at the US Open.

Needless to say, Ilie's request was denied. But surprisingly, it was reported the planes were rerouted later after many other complaints.

Clay Court problems. Most know not to erase out a ball mark on a clay court. If you erase the mark before the chair umpire has decided on whether the ball was in or out, you concede whatever the call was.

We all know that clay is the only surface that the umpire can make inspections. If playing on clay, and although it is tempting, it's not a good idea to instantly go over to the other side the check a disputed mark.

Tennis Quiz Question #8

You must wear sunglasses on sunny days since eye protection is more important than winning or losing. Correct?

A. Sunglasses aren't required but you would be wise to use them to avoid harmful UV rays.

B. Not required, but they make you feel cool.

C. Both A and B are correct.

(The answer is on p. 99)

(The answer is on p. 99)

Want 9.7 more years to your life? The Copenhagen City Heart Study (CCHS) did a study where they followed about 9,000 people over 25 years and found that playing tennis added 9.7 years to their lives.

Here is a brief excerpt from their findings. "There was a clear correlation between social interaction (connecting with others and maintaining strong relationships) and longevity. Also, the physical demands and challenges of playing tennis (and most racquet sports) along with balance and mental strategy requirements of the sport, contributed to positive life-enhancing factors as well." [35]

Tennis sayings.

- "Talk with your racquet, play with your heart."

- "Hustle hit and never quit."

- "Hustle and heart set us apart."

- "You Got Served!"

- "Teamwork Makes The Dream Work."

- "Love is nothing in tennis but in life it's everything!"

Take that! Jeff Tarango was an excellent doubles player and was runner-up at the 1999 French Open men's doubles. But Jeff had a huge temper and was known for big outbursts during matches. At the French Open, Jeff got mad (as most would) when a serve he clearly thought was an ace was called out.

The French crowd, however, backed the umpire's call and Jeff yelled out to the crowd to "SHUT UP!"

The umpire then promptly issued a code violation to Jeff.

That got Jeff even more outraged, and he told the umpire, "You are the most corrupt official. I'm not playing anymore." Jeff walked off the court and lost the match by default.

The crazy part about this story is that when that umpire went back to the changing room after declaring Jeff in default, he came across Jeff's wife, Benedicte, who instantly slapped the umpire in the face.

She said, "If Jeff had done it, he would have been put out of tennis." Other wives say if it was a totally bad call they would have done that too, but perhaps just tell the guy off. But it's great to see a wife stand up for her husband

"What'd you say about my mother?" John McEnroe was taught to stand up for himself which he certainly did at times. His infamous "You cannot be serious" outrage at Wimbledon when he shouted those infamous words and eventually after calling in for the referee, he won his first-round match against Tim Gulliksen. The 1981 video of this incident is here > https://www.youtube.com/watch?v=ransFQVzf6c

It's a tough world out there and most people don't want to be pushed around, especially John.

At the 1990 Australian Open John was playing Swedish player Mikael Pernfors.

During the match, John got an early warning from the umpire for intimidating a lineswoman (he stood staring at her after a call), and he was also docked a point for smashing a racket and shouting at a fan in the crowd whose baby was crying.

The tournament supervisor came onto the scene.

John got steamed again and said a few verbal obscenities to the tournament supervisor allegedly something vulgar about the supervisor's mother which the umpire clearly heard.

Within moments, the umpire announced "Verbal abuse, audible obscenity, default. game, set and match" giving Pernfors the win.

Taking charge! A man was getting his annual physical exam and his doctor asked him, "Do you engage in any dangerous sport?"

The man thought a bit, then said, "Well, sometimes I disagree with my wife."

They both laughed. "Seriously, doctor, there are times when I feel like I'm being bossed around, well, almost bullied by my wife. Would you have any suggestions on how I can stop her from bossing me around?"

"You need to build up your self-esteem. Read this short pamphlet on being assertive, and we'll talk further about it at the next appointment," the doctor said.

The man read it on the bus home and finished reading it just as he got off at his stop.

Storming through the front door of his house he walked right up to his wife and put his angry face an inch away from her face shouting, "Starting today, and I mean right now, I am the man of this house and whatever I say goes! And you've got nothing to say about it and I don't want to hear complaints or anything otherwise from you! None!"

The wife was startled.

He continued, "Starting right now, you are going to prepare an excellent dinner and when I'm finished, I will expect a beautiful dessert. When you are finished with that you are going into the garage and wash my tennis clothes and clean my tennis shoes and I don't want any stains or spots on them. Do you fully understand me?"

The wife stood motionless now shaking a bit like a volcano about to erupt.

"I'm playing tennis at the club after work, and I'll be hope at 6pm and expect you to have a warm bath ready for me. And, when I'm finished with my bath, guess who's going to dress me and comb my hair?"

"I think the funeral director's embalmers will be doing that," replied the wife.

It's not us, it's the court! In the 2002 Bausch & Lomb Championships at Amelia Island Plantation in Florida, the groundsman was very experienced since he'd been doing court preparation for 22 years. But he must have had something on his mind when he mistakenly miscalculated distances. It was an honest mistake.

The mistake involved the court having incorrect distances from the net to the service line, and from the service line to the baseline.

The correct distances are supposed to be 21 feet from the net to the service line and 18 feet to the baseline.

The groundsman, however, for some unknown reason flipped those figures and made it 18 feet from the net to the service line and 21 feet to the baseline.

So, the obvious happened in the match between Anne Kremer and Jennifer Hopkins playing a first-round match on the erroneously measured Stadium Court. They had a total of 29 double faults! After they complained to officials the mistake was discovered.

Romance on the court many years ago. Going back to Cannes, France in the year 1926, a large crowd gathered for tickets to watch French player Suzanne Lenglen play American Helen Wills who at that time was a strong up-and-coming player.

There was a close finish where Suzanne thought she had won but the English linesman Lord Hope said he had not called Helen's shot 'Out'.

Suzanne eventually won three games later and jubilant fans cheered and cheered for the popular French player.

However, Helen remained alone on the tennis court and was approached by Frederick Moody who complimented her on her performance.

Several years later she became Helen Wills-Moody and won 31 Grand Slam tournament titles during her career playing singles, doubles, and mixed doubles, including 19 singles titles. [36]

Comparisons. "The only player you should compare yourself to is the one you used to be."

-- Anon.

"Just trying to keep it fair?" The 1972 Davis Cup final between Romania and the US allegedly involved suspect officials. For example, in the match between Stan Smith vs. Ion Tiriac where Stan won in five sets, Stan was called on for foot faults repeatedly especially when he served aces. And Ion was egging on the crowd for noises to put Stan off.

However, what really was an unusual display of impartiality, one of the linesmen in front of the entire crowd massaged Tiriac's leg when he cramped up. To top that, the linesman was seen cheering Tiriac on to beat Stan!

No sense of humor. "I have no sense of humor in losing."

-- Rafael Nadal

Italians can be tennis casual. During the Italian championships in Rome in 1963, Tony Pickard, who was a very well-known British Davis Cup player, was playing a New Zealander Ian Crookenden.

It wasn't an exciting match and a bit boring but there was an unusual incident that Tony described, "It was a vital game point and Ian served and it was at least nine inches long. The umpire looked at the baseline judge for the call, but the baseline judge didn't see the serve since he was looking the other way and buying an ice cream from a vendor over the fence."

Ian won the point and eventually the match.

"I still got it!" In 1969, at the age of 41, Poncho Gonzales had a match with the up-and-coming and much younger Charlie Pasarell. Poncho won 22-24, 1-6, 16-14, 6-3, 11-9.

They played for 5 hours and 20 minutes, and a total of 112 games in the 5 sets. Pasarell reached match point 7 times, while Poncho was so tired he could hardly hold his racket, yet he saved himself two times from 0-40.

Poncho developed leg cramps in the final set and was moving only when necessary. However, Poncho had coached Pasarell and knew his weaknesses.

Poncho was exhausted when the last set began leaning on his racket at the start of the last set. He repeatedly leaned on his racket and was slightly staggering.

At 4-5 in the final set, Gonzales was 0-40 on his service and Pasarell was beginning to lob again as he successfully did in the opening two sets. This game went to deuce seven times.

At 5-6, Poncho was down at 0-40 again and it was difficult to tell if Poncho would be able to finish. Pasarell had another match point (his 7th) but hit a lob out.

Poncho seemed to gain a second wind and Pasarell lost 11 points in a row to lose the match.

Poncho Gonzales

No net. "Writing free verse without rhyme

Is like playing tennis without a net."

> -- Robert Frost

Understanding tennis.

"Doing tennis is something most people do not understand.

"Most think it's a sport. But it's not just a sport or something casual you do on a weekend,

"It's a way of living life.

"Once you're in it, it's in your blood.

"Once you hit your first winner or cracked your first ace, hit your first through your legs, or won your first match or tournament it's in your blood forever.

"The court becomes a home away from home and a tournament becomes more than an activity but rather a life-changing event.

"When you feel a clean winner off your racket, and hear the sound of the ball,

"You know you are home."

-- Anon.

A few tennis facts – not really!

Tennis was invented in 1979 to recreate the video game Pong in a 3D environment.

The grunting noises made by some female tennis players are added afterward by TV producers to annoy elderly viewers.

Tennis Grand Slams are played on three surfaces. Hard courts (US Open and Australia Open), Clay (French Open), and rain (Wimbledon).

Tennis Quiz Question #9.

You are playing on a windy day and your opponent puts backspin on his shot. The ball barely clears the net to your side of the court, then bounces back on his side, bounces and he can't hit it back. Your point?

A. Not your point since the wind speed must equal or exceed 40 mph for this to be your point.

B. His point since you must hit the ball with your racket to return it legally.

C. Your point since it is illegal to spin the ball that much.

(The answer is on p. 99)

Talking peanuts. Joe finished his usual Friday afternoon tennis game and walks over to the club bar. He notices a basket of roasted peanuts in the shell in front of him.

He reaches for one, then hears a voice, "You are amazing, Joe, you were smashing your serves, and your forehand shots were smokin'! You're the man! Oh, you're good looking too."

Joe pulls his hand back and takes a sip of beer wondering about what just happened. He tries to get another peanut and hears, "Your backhands were amazing, and you played down the lines so well! Have you've been working out and the bulk-up looks great on you!"

Then he hears several voices, "That's Joe! What a guy! He's smooth and smart! Women want him! What a catch he is!"

Joe looks over at the bartender and says, "What the hell? There are voices coming out of the peanut basket?!"

The bartender says, "Don't worry about it. The peanuts are complimentary."

Tennis Etiquette

You probably could add a few to these,

- More consideration to your opponents and to those waiting to play.

- Shorten warm-up time.

- Avoid all unnecessary delays.

- Be ready when it's your turn to receive service.

- Obey all the posted rules and observe proper etiquette.

Then on the more serious side, there is in existence "The Unwritten Rules of Tennis" USTA Rules and Regulations, Part 3, that sets out rules as there are a number of things not specifically set forth in the official rules and these are covered by custom and tradition.

As the USTA describes it, "Custom dictates the standard procedures that players will use in reaching decisions. These are the reasons a code is needed."

Examples are "Courtesy is expected", "Points played in good faith are counted", and many more things like warm-up is not a practice session and warm up is expected and should last 5 to 10 minutes and that includes practice service.

Also, it is considered customary to give an opponent the benefit of doubt when there is no official present, or if you catch a ball before it bounces, it's considered in no matter where you are standing and many more.

There are 46 unwritten rules and you can find them here > https://www.usta.com/content/dam/usta/pdfs/2015_Code.pdf

Tennis's greatest tip. You won't be an adequate tennis player unless you have confidence in your ability. The secret to obtaining confidence is to be certain you are playing correctly and using your full potential. Learn to concentrate and remain relaxed. See your pro regularly for a check-up.

It's like life. Life is like a game of tennis. The player who can serve well doesn't often lose."

-- Anon.

When I play tennis

No matter what,

It brings out the deepest

Passion, fire, drive, and desire.

After I step foot

On that magical court,

It is now my home,

I do not want to leave.

I spend every spare second

Of my time on that court

With a racket in hand and a bucket of balls

Making irreplaceable memories.

The court is my home.

You will have to drag me off.

That feeling is what passion is.

So, play with love, passion, and fire

And know you are making

The best memories of your life,

No matter the outcome of your match,

Or how bad you played at practice.

This is tennis a

A tradition that forms memories.

       -- Anon.

Tennis Question #10.

During a doubles match, you return serve, but the ball bounces off your partner's head. After hitting your partner in the head, the ball continues over the net to the other side of the court. Your partner stumbles and drops to the ground. The opposing team tries to return it but can't. They nevertheless claim the point. Are they right?

A. Your point. They would only get the point if your partner was still on his feet and did not fall.

B. Their point. There is no "assistance" in tennis like soccer or basketball.

C. Who cares? Get your partner medical attention right away.

(The answer is on p. 99)

Served yet? A tennis ball rolls into a bar. The barman asks, "Have you been served?"

The tennis ball stops and replies, "Not sure, but I'm a bit fuzzy… Wait.., if I'd been served, I'd be on the other side of the bar."

Grass courts. Three Grand Slam Tournaments do switch surfaces at times, but Wimbledon is the only Grand Slam Tournament always played on the same surface – grass.

The U.S. Open has been played on three surfaces and it's the only Grand Slam that has changed surfaces three times.

As you know, a grass court is the fastest surface and favors a serve and volley player. Balls also bounce low on grass and points are usually short.

Roger Federer is probably one of the greatest grass-court players the game has ever seen. He's won an amazing eight Wimbledon titles.

Roger Federer with Wimbledon Trophy

Tennis excuses.

- I got to get a new racket.

- They cheated.

- They hit everything back.

- The net must be too high.

- The sun was in my eyes.

- The wind took it.

- My hands are sweaty.

- You got a lucky bounce.

- Nick Kyrgios had a novel excuse when he lost to Federer in the Laver Cup. Nick said, "I lost concentration. I saw a really hot chick in the crowd. Like I'm being jarringly honest – I'd marry her right now. Right now!"

Bathroom walls. While sitting on the toilet, you see written on the stall door: Congratulations! You've won a free game of Toilet Tennis! Look Left.

You look left, and it reads: Look Right. You look right, and it reads: Look Left…

The good thing about losing. "If you don't lose, you cannot enjoy the victories. So, I have to accept both things."

   -- Rafael Nadal

Tennis's Greatest Lesson. Forget the past. Concentrate on the worthwhile new problems as they occur…optimistically i.e., forget the last bad shot or call.

Follow through on your life's goals. Finish your swing. Don't give up!

End of the match. "No matter if I win or lose, I give my opponent the hardest handshake I can.

If I lost I gave him a hard handshake to tell him I'd be back the next time.

If I won, I would give him that same hard handshake to show him I was strong and played the best I could."

   -- Wayne Ferreira

Stronger. "I always believe if you're stuck in a hole and maybe things aren't going well you will come out stronger. Everything in life is this way."

   -- Roger Federer.

Journey. "Success is a journey, not a destination. The doing is often more important than the outcome."

-- Arthur Ashe.

The one thing. "There is one huge thing that tennis has taught us is that being a champion is not just about winning or losing, it's about the fighting spirit within each of us. And it's a tough world out there where you need at times to show your fighting spirit."

-- Anon.

Great fight. "When the last point is done, we are humans. Give your opponent a hug and say, 'great fight,' and that's all."

- Novak Djokovic

Answers to Tennis Rule Questions

1. C
2. A
3. C
4. B
5. B
6. A
7. C
8. C
9. B
10. B

We hope you enjoyed our book!

If you liked our book, we would sincerely appreciate your taking a few moments to leave a brief review.

Thank you again very much!

TeamGolfwell and Bruce Miller

Bruce@TeamGolfwell.com

About the authors

Bruce Miller. Lawyer, businessman, world traveler, golf enthusiast, Golf Rules Official, TVC actor, and author of over 50 books, a few being Amazon bestsellers, spends his days writing, studying, and constantly learning of the astounding, unexpected, and amazing events happening in the world today while exploring the brighter side of life. He is a member of Team Golfwell, Authors, and Publishers.

Team Golfwell are bestselling authors and founders of the very popular 300,000+ member Facebook Group "Golf Jokes and Stories." Their books have sold thousands of copies including several #1 bestsellers in Golf Coaching, Sports humor, and other categories.

We Want to Hear from You!

"There usually is a way to do things better and there is opportunity when you find it." - *Thomas Edison*

We love to hear your thoughts and suggestions on anything and please feel free to contact us at Bruce@TeamGolfwell.com

Other Books by Bruce Miller [37] and Team Golfwell [38]

Brilliant Screen-Free Stuff to Do with Kids: A Handy Reference for Parents & Grandparents!

For the Golfer Who Has Everything: A Funny Golf Book

For the Mother Who Has Everything: A Funny Book for Mother

For the Father Who Has Everything: A Funny Book for Father

For the Grandmother Who Has Everything: A Funny Book for Grandmothers

For the Grandfather Who Has Everything: A Funny Book for Grandfathers

The Funniest Quotations to Brighten Every Day: Brilliant, Inspiring, and Hilarious Thoughts from Great Minds

Jokes for Very Funny Kids (Ages 3 to 7): Funny Jokes, Riddles and More

Jokes for Very Funny Kids (Big & Little): Funny Jokes and Riddles Ages 9 - 12 and up and many more. [39]

For a Great Fisherman Who Has Everything: A Funny Book for Fishermen

And many more…

Index

References

[1] Michelle Larcher de Brito, Wikipedia, https://en.wikipedia.org/wiki/Michelle_Larcher_de_Brito#Grunting_controversy

[2] Ibid.

[3] Center for Disease Control, Loud Noise Can Cause Hearing Loss, https://www.cdc.gov/nceh/hearing_loss/what_noises_cause_hearing_loss.html

[4] Vanderbilt Tennis Club, https://vanderbilttennisclub.com/

[5] Fastest recorded tennis serves, https://en.wikipedia.org/wiki/Fastest_recorded_tennis_serves

[6] The Guardian, https://www.theguardian.com/sport/2014/jul/30/sabine-lisicki-record-fastest-serve-women-tennis-stanford

[7] Ibid.

[8] YouTube, https://www.youtube.com/watch?v=rCKWA2BLFO4

[9] Britannica Encyclopedia, Tennis,
https://www.britannica.com/sports/tennis
[10] Ibid.
[11] Ibid.
[12] Tennis Balls, Wikipedia,
https://en.wikipedia.org/wiki/Tennis_ball#History
[13] Tennis ball, Wikipedia,
https://en.wikipedia.org/wiki/Tennis_ball
[14] Ibid.
[15] Tennis de la Cavalerie
http://www.tennisdelacavalerie.com/lieu_historique
[16] List of most visited palaces and monuments, Wikipedia,
https://en.wikipedia.org/wiki/List_of_most_visited_palaces_and_monuments
[17] Ibid.
[18] Tennis ball, Wikipedia,
https://en.wikipedia.org/wiki/Tennis_ball
[19] Ibid.
[20] Stan Wawrinka, Wikipedia,
https://en.wikipedia.org/wiki/Stan_Wawrinka
[21] Novak Djokovic, YouTube,
https://www.youtube.com/watch?v=sUtQadqgxZo
[22] Jimmy Van Alen, Wikipedia,
https://en.wikipedia.org/wiki/Jimmy_Van_Alen
[23] The Sun, thesun.co.uk/sport/15365388/john-mcenroe-tennis-wimbledon-bjorn-borg/
[24] King James I Assassination, Wikipedia,
https://en.wikipedia.org/wiki/James_I_of_Scotland#Assassination
[25] ATP Tour.com, https://www.atptour.com/en/news/how-carlos-alcaraz-has-built-a-winning-team
[26] Ibid.
[27] Shortest tennis match records, Wikipedia,
https://en.wikipedia.org/wiki/Shortest_tennis_match_records

[28] List of tennis stadiums by capacity, Wikipedia, https://en.wikipedia.org/wiki/List_of_tennis_stadiums_by_ca pacity

[29] Goran Ivanišević, Wikipedia, https://en.wikipedia.org/wiki/Goran_Ivani%C5%A1evi%C4% 87

[30] Ibid.

[31] Ibid.

[32] NTNews, https://www.ntnews.com.au/sport/how-boris-beckers-slip-of-the-tongue-gave-andre-agassi-the-upper-hand-in-their-rivalry/news-story/b731c42f1df3826874f61a0fece55a28

[33] The Daily Star, "I was grouped by a ghost, https://www.dailystar.co.uk/showbiz/casey-batchelor-manor-house-ghost-19199216

[34] Ibid.

[35] USTA, Mayo Clinic, https://www.usta.com/es/content/dam/usta/sections/northern/p df/hainline-interview/tennis-benefits-mayo.pdf

[36] Helen Wills, Wikipedia, https://en.wikipedia.org/wiki/Helen_Wills

[37] https://www.amazon.com/Bruce-Miller/e/B096C9SN2R?

[38] https://www.amazon.com/Team-Golfwell/e/B01CFW4EQG?

[39] Ibid.